PURSUING THE GOD OF HOPE® POETRY SERIES

Sacred Space

Danita Kay

Sacred Space

Published by Four Winds Publishing
© 2019, Danita Kay

Library of Congress Cataloging-in-Publication Data is on file
at the Library of Congress, Washington, D.C.

ISBN: 978-1-7335770-0-7 paperback

Photography and illustration credits are listed on page 66
and constitute an extension of this copyright page.

Scripture quotations labeled NKJV are from the New King James
Version of the Bible.

Scripture quotations labeled GNT are from the Holy Bible,
Good News Translation. Copyright © 1992 by American Bible
Society. Used by permission of American Bible Society.
All rights reserved worldwide.

Layout and production by Author

To My Friends—

Miss Ivy Duncan & Miss Edna Mae Morris,
two kindred souls and spiritual role models.
May you both rest in peace.

❧ ❦

"Eternity sits before us and still we seem to rebel at the voice of God, failing to entirely realize the power of His name (El Shaddai). Somehow, though, I know that in spite of each misstep or fall from grace, I am—we all are—even nearer our most precious, eternal God and shelter. Meanwhile, we journey toward Him, along sacred pathways leading to a variety of 'thin places' that propel us forward, toward eternity."

-- Danita

Table of Contents

SACRED MOMENTS

(Pursuing the God of Hope)

As the deer pants for the water brooks,
So pants my soul for You, O God.
² My soul thirsts for God, for the living God.
When shall I come and appear before God?
³ My tears have been my food day and night,
While they continually say to me,
"Where *is* your God?"

⁴ When I remember these *things,*
I pour out my soul within me.
For I used to go with the multitude;
I went with them to the house of God,
With the voice of joy and praise,
With a multitude that kept a pilgrim feast.

⁵ Why are you cast down, O my soul?
And *why* are you disquieted within me?
Hope in God, for I shall yet praise Him
For the help of His countenance.

⁶ O my God, my soul is cast down within me;
Therefore I will remember You from the land of the Jordan,
And from the heights of Hermon,
From the Hill Mizar.
⁷ Deep calls unto deep at the noise of Your waterfalls;
All Your waves and billows have gone over me.
⁸ The LORD will command His lovingkindness in the daytime,
And in the night His song *shall be* with me—
A prayer to the God of my life.

⁹ I will say to God my Rock,
"Why have You forgotten me?
Why do I go mourning because of the oppression of the enemy?"
¹⁰ *As* with a breaking of my bones,
My enemies reproach me,
While they say to me all day long,
"Where *is* your God?"

¹¹ Why are you cast down, O my soul?
And why are you disquieted within me?
Hope in God;
For I shall yet praise Him,
The help of my countenance and my God.

Psalm 42 (KJV)

The dead goldfinch, "All that was left to love"
By George Elgar Hicks

I'm well acquainted with sorrow
but never at home with her kind
(though she likes to visit at will)
I have never pursued her friendship
or led her to believe she's welcome.
thanks to my turns with sorrow,
I know only Love can conquer grief,
It's Love that steadies your hand to
mine the ruins of a shattered heart
(to see what truly brings peace).
It's Love alone that lifts the feet
as you step forward through life
toward joy—and better tomorrows
It is only Love that will allow
A pain-stricken heart to have hope.

❧ ❧

While watching a PBS special on the life of Zora Neale Hurston some years ago, a quote of hers caught my attention. Like the character Much Afraid in "Hinds' Feet on High Places," I believe Ms. Hurston allowed the tutoring of her soul by sorrow and suffering to bring about a transformation facilitated by God's grace. Thus, she would eventually declare beautifully.:

"I have been in Sorrow's kitchen and licked out all the pots.
Then I have stood on the peaky mountain wrapped in rainbows,
with a harp and a sword in my hands."

--Zora Neale Hurston

My interpretation of Ms. Hurston's quote: "I have not confined myself to sorrow's kitchen—to the constant reopening of old wounds. I have stepped outside of my circumstances to experience the joy of coming through it all. I have reached beyond the pain and experienced the promises of God, with a song in my heart and His word in my hand." Psalm 27:13 comes to mind:

"I would have lost heart, unless I had believed that
I would see the goodness of the Lord in the land of the living."

--Psalm 27:13

Many a man awakes
to the dawn of a new day
some to bitter fruit;
others, a sun ray.
dusk, dawn,
the once-again-born
to everything
there is a season,
and a time
for everything under the sun
from dust man came
and to dust he'll return
be it summer, fall,
winter or spring.

to *everything*
there is a season
and a time ...
a time to live,
a time to die,
a time to laugh,
a time to cry

Many a tear flow
throughout the night,
some because of death;
others, fright.
still, men awake
to the dawn of a new day
some new in Christ,
others fixed in sin.

dusk, dawn, sunsets, and storms
life, death, to be born-again ...

joy comes, still,
in the morning.

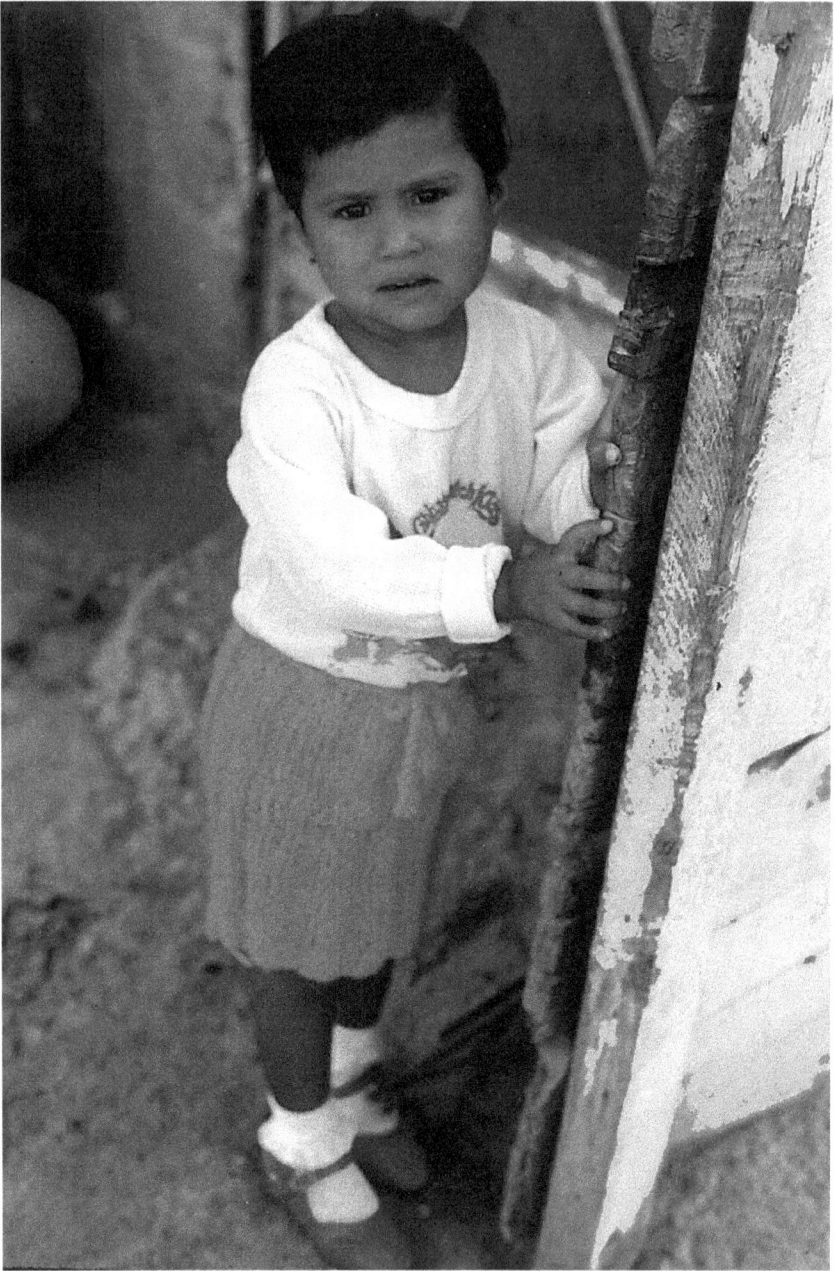

Young girl in Monterey, Mexico (1992)

⟨⟩ ∞

"Incorruptible Treasures"

[3] "Blessed be the God and Father of our Lord Jesus Christ, the Father of mercies and God of all comfort, [4] who comforts us in all our tribulation, that we may be able to comfort those who are in any [a]trouble, with the comfort with which we ourselves are comforted by God. [5] For as the sufferings of Christ abound in us, so our [b]consolation also abounds through Christ." -- II Corinthians 1:3-5

I first embarked upon missions abroad during the fall of '92 when I visited Mexico. While in Mexico, I met a little boy who lived in a poor area of Monterey. He was a quiet, gentle child who immediately attached himself to me. Even now, I really can't figure out the moment we first made contact. He was just there. Whenever I moved or turned, there was this little boy who seemed to be waiting for something. At the same time, he really seemed content just being near me.

In the awkwardness of realizing another occupying my personal space, I attempted to reach out in an effort to somehow soothe him in some tiny way. I asked him his name. He said, "Juan." I told him my name. He hung around a while. Before he left, I gave him three dollars.

I continue the work that we'd come to Mexico to do. Some time passed since Juan had left us. To my surprise, he returned bearing gifts for me! His gesture was beyond touching given his lack of financial security. He'd bought me a doll and Coke. I thanked him, and he hung out with us the rest of that day. I sensed that he was satisfied just having me stroke his hair as my other arm rested upon his small shoulders.

When it was time for us to leave his expression became so sad—so unexplainably sad. He stood on the porch of a home and just stared sad-eyed and sorrowful.

"I don't know what else to do," I said to a fellow missionary after exchanging addresses with him.

"There's nothing else you can do," she replied, urging me to just walk on.

We both sensed a deep longing for something beyond our current ability to fulfill. Yet, I know that what we sensed was really a spiritual hunger he sensed our presence could ease. A hunger I'm sure he didn't understand, but one that he realized was satiated by the message we shared.

My experience with Juan brings to mind a question often asked in response to God's call to "go forth" onto the mission field:

"What difference can I make anyway; my going won't save this world and my not going won't cause it to end either?"

Today, my response to the question regarding "making a difference" is new. I must reply that I know in my heart that I've made a difference in at least three lives. And though I may have made no difference on any given day with regard to immediately changing the world, God's word promises that:

> *"...Eye hath not seen, nor ear heard, neither have entered into the heart of man, the things which God hath prepared for them that love him."*
> -- I Cor. 2:9

How does any one of us at any time know to what extent our life—or any life we've encountered or touched in some way—may have monumental impact on this world?

How do we know to what extent our being in Mexico on that particular day might play a role in Juan's life being transformed by the power of God? How can we know what role our influence will have on any one of the others present?

We don't know. We may never know to what extent our touching a life may affect the world. Any one we minister to can at some point in the future become a solution to a global problem. The realm of possibilities is unimaginable by the human mind.

I went to Mexico because I wanted to become a more effective witness of Christ's existence and love; because I wanted to actually *"see"* His Word come alive in the people we would meet. I came away realizing that my presence on the mission field was more than an opportunity to give to those we ministered to.

It is in our pursuit of God that we encounter opportunities to encourage others in pursuit of Him also. I learned that missionaries provide those who are often less fortunate in many ways an opportunity to share whatever they can. Many of the people we served enjoyed the chance to give--enjoyed an opportunity to experience the joy of "reaching out" to us. Many, like Juan, get to give of all they actually possess themselves.

We received an incorruptible treasure in return for obeying God. We received the love of a human soul who is not only introduced to a hope that is Christ the living God, but a soul that also realizes a tangible reflection of that hope in us.

CB BO

I sit

in self-emptying exile,

(a journey of faith)

as God puts to death

childish things

in order to resurrect

something new.

I seek

to find the place

of my revival

as I imagine . . .

metaphorical images

of that mansion

in the sky—

stone huts

housing beehives

of golden honey

and more

—built by

the King of us all

(and the elements),

true originator

of the phrase

    "Semper Fi".

SACRED PRAYER

(Talking to the God of Hope)

C₃ 80

⁵ "When you pray, do not be like the hypocrites! They love to stand up and pray in the houses of worship and on the street corners, so that everyone will see them. I assure you, they have already been paid in full. ⁶ But when you pray, go to your room, close the door, and pray to your Father, who is unseen. And your Father, who sees what you do in private, will reward you.

⁷ "When you pray, do not use a lot of meaningless words, as the pagans do, who think that their gods will hear them because their prayers are long. ⁸ Do not be like them. Your Father already knows what you need before you ask him. ⁹ This, then, is how you should pray:

> *Our Father which art in heaven,*
> *Hallowed be thy name.*
> *Thy kingdom come,*
> *Thy will be done*
> *in earth, as it is in heaven.*
> *Give us this day our daily bread.*
> *And forgive us our debts,*
> *as we forgive our debtors.*
> *And lead us not into temptation,*
> *but deliver us from evil:*
> *For thine is the kingdom,*
> *and the power,*
> *and the glory,*
> *for ever. Amen.*

Matthew 6 (GNT)

King Saul

Save me from bitterness, God, I plead.
No, I prefer the pleader's chance,
prefer to beg and crawl.
Not as though I were too cold to bleed,
not as though I were above circumstance
to escape a bloody brawl.

If I were once again at peace,
oh, no longer ill at ease
among kinfolk, thick as thieves!
I would sing of Your love forever
and stand firm in faith, and endeavor
not to be ruled by carnal needs.

God forbid! One choosing bitterness
would be revealed by countenance,
and very soon be disgraced,
relegated to a life of hatefulness,
and, as upon the wild beast Saul
all would stare amazed . . .

For in the gloom of such darkness I
would not tend to the will of my Lord,
and tug of His love or hand—
but to the prods of that enemy,
and repeated vows of revenge
(succumbing to red-hot rage)

CB ED

"Captured"

Christian music artist Nicole C. Mullen as well as other artists have had popular hit songs with lyrics centered on the experience of being "captured" by God. The idea of "being captured" brings to mind a story I was assigned to read for an English class. It is the story of Colón, a youngster without meaningful human guidance, yet a strong desire to lead a meaningful, purposeful (moral) existence. He is a person of conviction, principle, and seemingly fragile self-worth. Along with those factors, many others surround his difficulty living and working in New York City. First, he lives in poverty. He has no electricity, hence no heat, in a city of frigid weather. He exists in near despair, in seemingly hopeless circumstances.

Colón faces prejudice, racism, and discrimination and also shares in his people's struggle to somehow set themselves apart from their heritage with regard to workplace prejudices. When he does manage to obtain employment, Colón often works as slave labor (for less than 20 cents an hour) while bowing and scraping before his oppressors.

The thing of greatest value to Colón is of a material nature. He is a guy who possesses nothing of value except a poem—Rudyard Kipling's, *"If "*. It is a possession that he wants to share with others:

If you can keep your head when all about you
Are losing theirs and blaming it on you,
If you can trust yourself when all men doubt you,
But make allowance for their doubting too;
If you can wait and not be tired by waiting,
Or being lied about, don't deal in lies,
Or being hated, don't give way to hating,
And yet don't look too good, not talk too wise:

If you can dream—and not make dreams your master;
If you can think—and not make thoughts your aim;
If you can meet with Triumph and Disaster
And treat those two impostors just the same;
If you can bear to hear the truth you've spoken
Twisted by knaves to make a trap for fools,
Or watch the things you gave your life to, broken,
And stoop and build 'em up with worn-out tools:

If you can make one heap of all your winnings
And risk it on one turn of pitch-and-toss,
And lose, and start again at your beginnings
And never breathe a word about your loss;
If you can force your heart and nerve and sinew
To serve your turn long after they are gone,
And so hold on when there is nothing in you
Except the Will which says to them: 'Hold on!'

If you can talk with crowds and keep your virtue,
'Or walk with Kings—nor lose the common touch,
if neither foes nor loving friends can hurt you,
If all men count with you, but none too much;
If you can fill the unforgiving minute
With sixty seconds' worth of distance run,
Yours is the Earth and everything that's in it,
And—which is more—you'll be a Man, my son!

Colón comes off as being a bit obsessed with Kipling's words. The poem has become his personal mantra. It has become his idol, and is viewed by him somewhat as a magic charm of sorts. It is his daily devotional.

"Our hearts," writes Paula Rinehart, "can be captured by almost anything." She maintains that "addictions get their fuel from leeching off of our true desires." "Attachment," Rinehart maintains, "comes from the French word attaché, which means 'nailed to'. In addiction or attachment, our desires are nailed to a specific object." Rinehart views addiction as having one's heart "captured."[1] I'd never heard addiction defined this way. It's so true. The thought of having our hearts captured by someone or thing other than Him must provoke disheartening emotions in our Creator.

In the end, Colón burns the poem out of sheer necessity. He was freezing and without any resources to obtain warmth except his poem and its encasement. So, he destroyed that which had come to represent everything—destroyed a core part of his life in an effort to sustain it. What good is any material possession, ultimately, except that it is a means to some life-sustaining end?

"If I continue to peel back the layers of desire, I discover... the front edge of a longing for home. ... a place outside the material world that will always be there; where everything is secure and I know I am loved."[2]

* * * * * *

Lamentation

Of my wasted years the vanished song and laughter
haunts me like the deafening silence of disaster.
Not so red-hot rage—or so it seems to me,
that as days go by screams ever more loudly.
Few are the paths before me: death and life,
stretched along corridors of worldly hype.

And yet from thought of life, my lord, I wince;
I want sweet justice for others' every offense,
and amid suffering and grief and tribulation
taste also of Your presence—of divine retaliation;
Be drunk in the Spirit; grasp love's wings,
realizing beyond my highest imaginings . . .
all that God has in store for those who love Him,
my soul captured at last by hounds of heaven.

SACRED SILENCE

(Listening for the God of Hope)

Ezekiel 37:1-14

The hand of the LORD came upon me and brought me out in the Spirit of the LORD, and set me down in the midst of the valley; and it *was* full of bones. ² Then He caused me to pass by them all around, and behold, *there were* very many in the open valley; and indeed, *they were* very dry. ³ And He said to me, "Son of man, can these bones live?"

So I answered, "O Lord GOD, You know."

⁴ Again He said to me, "Prophesy to these bones, and say to them, 'O dry bones, hear the word of the LORD! ⁵ Thus says the Lord GOD to these bones: "Surely I will cause breath to enter into you, and you shall live. ⁶ I will put sinews on you and bring flesh upon you, cover you with skin and put breath in you; and you shall live. Then you shall know that I *am* the LORD.""'

⁷ So I prophesied as I was commanded; and as I prophesied, there was a noise, and suddenly a rattling; and the bones came together, bone to bone. ⁸ Indeed, as I looked, the sinews and the flesh came upon them, and the skin covered them over; but *there was* no breath in them.

⁹ Also He said to me, "Prophesy to the breath, prophesy, son of man, and say to the breath, 'Thus says the Lord GOD: "Come from the four winds, O breath, and breathe on these slain, that they may live."""' ¹⁰ So I prophesied as He commanded me, and breath came into them, and they lived, and stood upon their feet, an exceedingly great army.

¹¹ Then He said to me, "Son of man, these bones are the whole house of Israel. They indeed say, 'Our bones are dry, our hope is lost, and we ourselves are cut off!' ¹² Therefore prophesy and say to them, 'Thus says the Lord GOD: "Behold, O My people, I will open your graves and cause you to come up from your graves, and bring you into the land of Israel. ¹³ Then you shall know that I *am* the LORD, when I have opened your graves, O My people, and brought you up from your graves. ¹⁴ I will put My Spirit in you, and you shall live, and I will place you in your own land. Then you shall know that I, the LORD, have spoken *it* and performed *it*," says the LORD.'"

03 80

Eternity sits before us

And still we seem to

Rebel, at the voice of God,

Not appreciating His name

(El Shaddai) for all that it is.

C3 80

"His Mysterious Ways"

I was working in a convenience store on Cape Cod during the summer of '87 when an elderly woman walked up to purchase a gallon of milk. I don't remember who initiated our conversation, but I learned that she was in her eighties and Irish. She had immigrated to the states in the early '70s.

"You know, I'm going next door to get a bite to eat," she told me, "Would you mind terribly if I left my bags here until I finished?"

I thought her request a bit odd, but agreed to keep the items for her.

"Are you sure?" she asked, "Thank you so much?"

As the lady left the store, I stood for a moment, wondering about her request. "Oh, well," I finally thought, "maybe the jug of milk is too heavy for her to carry any distance." The fact that she'd also left her purse behind remained a mystery to me.

Sometime later I looked up to see the old woman at the counter, smiling. "I'm back. Thank-you ever so much," she said as I handed over her belongings. She stood before me, still smiling. "Jesus loves you," she then declared, "And, so do I!"

The words were spoken with such a melodic swing, such sincerity that I was taken back. The elderly patron had caught me off guard. I stood speechless before finally responding, "Oh....ok."

"Jesus loves me, and so does she," I thought to myself. The woman had said what appeared to me to be strange, yet I believed her.

Despite my natural tendency toward analyzing people and words for authenticity—in spite of the fact that she didn't know me, nor I her—I actually believed her. "It's crazy," I remember thinking, "but I believe she really meant what she said."

The woman left the store. Minutes later, however, I noticed her still standing outside. I decided to ask her if she was all right. She explained that she was ok, just waiting for a cab.

"Tell me," she asked, her eyes fixed upon mine. She was serious, yet smiling. "What do you want?"

I was taken by surprise once again, and stood silent—at a loss for words.

"I'm going to pray," she declared, placing her hand on my arm, "and ask God to give you whatever your heart desires."

"Ok," I said, once again perplexed yet appreciative of her kindness. I then went back inside to my work. I looked outside upon returning to my register and she was gone.

On the way home that afternoon, I stopped by the library. I had decided to stray somewhat from my usual path by going to Main Street so that I could walk home along Sea Street Beach. I sat down to rest once inside the library. While sitting, I recognized a book lying next to me. I'd seen it on a shelf in the hallway outside my room at the boarding house where I stayed. I picked up the book and opened it. My eyes landed on words that momentarily stopped by breathing. My heart was pounding. I sat still (spooked) . . . staring at the words:

"Jesus Loves You
And So Do I!"

My child, My child It is I within thee
Which causes you to long for me;
There is no need to worry or wonder,
No cause for fear as you ponder;

For I am with you all of the way,
Continue in my word from day to day;
No need to trouble yourself with doubt,
My love for you is what it's all about.

Thank you my child for your appeal,
As you inquire I will reveal
Walk in my statues and trust my word
Then you will know It's my voice you heard!

Continue to plant seeds on good ground,
You will then see me unfold all around;
I am the potter, you are the clay,
I mold and make you in my special way.

I reveal my will by the Holy Ghost,
For He alone knows your inner most.

[According to the Bible, the love of God is spread abroad through his holy spirit
that dwells within us. Thus, God often speaks to us through the creative works of
others. The above poem was penned by a dear friend, Ms. Edna Mae Morris in
response to one that I'd written in which I'd questioned God about various points.
Listening for the God of hope resulted in this heartfelt gift of love from one in
whom his spirit dwelled.]

Sojourn Beneath the Sky

Using a hair pin when only the Sword will do, hoping
       without faith, mistaking sand for pearl
       of great price; deceived by the whim and wiles of one
whom this world loves better than it loves you, God in you—

You have lived and died on every kind of shortage.
       You have been compelled to settle by kin
       and fair-weather friend, and have heard Him say:
"There is a carnal temperament in direct contrast to Mine,

which makes you do these things. Narrow is the way
       toward the promises and faith to
       receive, you will again yield to the hounds of heaven
and leave sin. Compelled by My love, you will turn back:

Eagles are created to soar
       And you have flown." An Eagle among turkeys
       cannot soar. Yet you see it, when the storms of
compromise blow with force, rise above it all.

My Dear Child,

Nothing in your self-concept or your past is too big
to keep you from reaching the goals I have set for you—
from your accomplishing My will for your life.
I have chosen, gifted, and accepted you.
Start to see yourself as I see you…
as one through whom I can change the world.

God.

SACRED PATHWAYS

(Worshipping the God of Hope)

Big Moon Rising

(A Poetic Harvest)

When there's a big moon rising, I watch it
lift above the Earth's edge, and I know that
God sits above us, directing the nocturnal
display of twinkling stars—the orb of light.

I wonder whether 'Big Bang' theorists shall
ever come to know the Creator of galaxies
or truly grasp the grand design from which
all things transpire, fade and flow?

Whenever there's a big moon rising, I will
head outdoors with my trusty iPod in hand,
extend a bud to the ear of God and to mine
then dance joyfully under a nighttime sky.

Cʒ ᵇᴼ

"A Healer of Chickens"

*"It is the definition of joy to be able to offer back to God
the essence of what he's placed in you, be that creativity or a love
of ideas or a compassionate heart or the gift of hospitality."*[3]

L ike the monk described in Becket's "American Monk," the pathway to worshiping God for many is through nature. When I think of the *Naturalists*, Ms. Ivy Duncan comes to mind. Ms. Ivy was an octogenarian from Jamaica who became one of my best friends. She was a retired nurse, dedicated Christian and vocal advocate of drinking an adequate amount of water daily, without fail. Although we never broached the subject of worshiping styles, I believe that she must have been a naturalist. First, the application of her nursing skills wasn't limited to humans. She told me that she was quite successful as a healer of chickens back home in Jamaica.

During the early 90's a friend from church informed me that her parents were moving to the area to live out their retirement. At some point thereafter, I offered to assist her mom with raking leaves at their home. I showed up for work and met an elderly woman possessing a merry heart and an abundance of energy. I became exhausted raking leaves on an extremely humid day. She outlasted me by at least an hour, and only stopped working after my insisting that we take a break and get a drink of water.

By offering to assist Ms. Ivy with yard work, I gained a great friend and many opportunities to experience Jamaican cuisine. I was introduced to various foods for the first time, including: oxtail stew, catfish stew, a ginger drink and callaloo.

My dear friend was a tough, adventurous soul. She visited my home once to gather figs from our tree. While doing so, I looked up to see her perched above me gathering figs. To my horror, she'd climbed the tree. I insisted that she come down immediately. Thoughts of explaining a fall to her daughters terrified me. How could I have allowed an eighty-plus-year-old-woman climb a tree?

Ms. Ivy and I tilled soil in her backyard to prepare a plot for callaloo plants. She planted a variety of trees through the years, including lemon trees, which I got to see reach about twenty feet tall. Along with my love of gardening, Ms. Ivy and I also had in common the practice of writing out our prayers to God. We both wrote poetry and prayers. We discussed the possibility of compiling hers into a book one day and publishing it.

I so admired Ms. Ivy's devotion to God and Christ-like living. She was Catholic and her determination to attend mass each morning despite her age and disability was remarkable. Even with a leg bent outward as a result of childhood polio, my dear friend would walk a half mile to church on some mornings (when her ride didn't show up as soon as she would have liked it to). She would trek from her home, along a major (shoulder-less) thoroughfare that dropped off on both sides into four feet deep ditches, then cross often horrific morning traffic.

Ms. Ivy Duncan was definitely a "soul friend" whose presence in my life drew me closer to God. Hanging out with her provided a brief retreat from the vexations of day-to-day living. We talked about many things.

We did a bit of gardening. She especially strived to drive home the importance of maintaining one's health, and would occasionally share articles from health newsletters that she subscribed to.

I particularly recall her words during a past "dark night of the soul" I'd experienced. I asked her about her easy-going manner—her modest ways. I inquired whether she'd always been so calm and unflappable. She told me that she had not always been. Ms. Ivy told me about a time in her young life when she became so angry that she was physically blinded by her rage. She had promised God then that if He restored her sight, she would never again allow herself to become consumed by anger. And so, she'd diligently kept her promise.

It seemed that God had in that moment offered the testimony of this lovely lady to combat my hearts pain. Hearing her story had suddenly snapped me out of grief I'd been experiencing. It was as if I'd been awakened from my sorrow by the realization that someone I'd respected had been there too, had been so wronged and yet survived in a miraculous state of Christ-likeness. I could thus more easily believe that it was possible for things to get better. I realized that even dark nights of the soul can by grace be transformed into a most sacred space.

03 80

I sit
listening
to the lovely
tinkling
of sea-worn rocks,
braving the tempest
of oceanic nature.
I wonder,
what does it all mean?
and I think
of our need to come
face to face
with the abrasive
nature of life itself
lest we be tempted
to entertain
idealistic notions
about delightful things
that alienate us
from God.

"I like the idea that God was thinking of me long before I was born—that He considered me when He so intricately planned then formed all of creation. I can only imagine the pleasure He must have experienced as He looked ahead and saw my amazement at His artistry—at nature, foreign cultures and lands, and revelations of Him!"

-Danita

Father great is thy faithfulness

(A Poetic Harvest)

to create a sacred space,
where heart-felt heaviness
(so much suffering) often exists.
Lord, do not hand over the life
of your dove to the wild beasts.

Be Thou mine in ordinary ways
for I seek God, Jesus, and Holy Spirit
as I rise in holy occupation,
with right actions, in prayer,
as I rise in celebration of Christ's
immanence—part of this mystery
(the living reality) of the Trinity.

May the road rise to meet me
and streams of living water
flow throughout my veins
as I drink from the well of Your grace,
as I yield to *Your* will through prayer
(and the resurrection it brings).

From dark to dark I'll praise Thee
with God-honoring prayers
I'll dwell upon the earth
(all God's domain) praising
"Hosanna to God in the Highest"
"Hosanna Forever!"
For You alone are worthy
of a thunderous ovation of praise!

ENDNOTES

[1] Paula Rinehart. Strong Women, Soft Hearts (Nashville: Thomas Nelson Publishers, 2005), 28

[2] Rinehart, 29.

[3] Rinehart, 24

PHOTO CREDITS

Review Request

I hope that you enjoyed this book!

෴

If so, would you please leave an honest review on Amazon?

Thank You!

https://amazon.com/author/danitakay

Other Books by Author:

Sojourn Beneath the Sky

❧ ❧

Cabbage Patch Meals

Farm Babies

Lettuce Eat!

"M" is for Mama

❧ ❧

amazon.com/author/danitakay

www.ingramcontent.com/pod-product-compliance
Lightning Source LLC
Chambersburg PA
CBHW071848020426
42331CB00007B/1918